A LATE SNOW

"A well-crafted play with three-dimensional characters, rich humor, a believable story line and important statements."
—THE CONNECTION

"Combines humor, decency and honesty with intelligent observations about the nature of human relationships . . . very, very funny."
—NEW YORK THEATRE VOICE

"An important breakthrough . . . moving and convincing."
—LOS ANGELES TIMES

"An important play that should be seen by everyone, straight, gay or on the fringe."

—DRAMA-LOGUE

"One warm wonderful play."

—NEW YORK NATIVE

A LATE SNOW, the Meridian Gay Theatre revival: (l-r) Pamela Osowski, Kathryn Shield, Jere Jacob and Maggie Suter. (Photo Terry Miller)

A LATE SNOW

a play in two acts

by Jane Chambers

THE JH PRESS GAY PLAY SCRIPT SERIES

JH PRESS
Box 294, Village Station
New York, N.Y. 10014-0294

Copyright © 1970 by Jane Chambers

Cover design: Nancy Johnson, Aenjai Graphic Studio
Back cover photo: Beth Allen

First JH Press edition, January 1989

Library of Congress Cataloging-in-Publications Data

Chambers, Jane, 1937-1983
    A late snow: a play by Jane Chambers.
       p. cm.—(The JH Press gay play script series)
    ISBN 0-935672-14-1: $6.95
    I. Title. II. Series.
PS3553.H258L34   1988   812'.54   88-13294
                                                                   CIP

A LATE SNOW was produced at the Clark Center for the Performing Arts, in 1974. Produced by Playwrights Horizons; directed by Nyla Lyon; costumes by Sally Blankfield; lighting design by Patrika Brown. In the original cast:

```
QUINCEY .. Carolyn Cope (replaced by Lin Shaye)
PAT ............................ Susan Sullivan
ELLIE ......................... Susanne Wasson
MARGO .......................... Anita Keal
PEGGY ........................ Marilyn Hamlin
```

A LATE SNOW was revived by Meridian Gay Theatre, Terry Helbing and Terry Miller, producers, at the Urban Arts Theatre, opening September 15, 1983. Directed by Francine L. Trevens; scenic design by Leon Munier; lighting design by Peter Anderson; costume/prop coordination by Lynn Marrapodi; assistant director: Jeannine Haas; stage manager: Janine Trevens.

```
QUINCEY ...................... Kathryn Shield
PAT ................................ Jere Jacob
ELLIE ........................... Maggie Suter
MARGO .................... Pamela H. Osowski
PEGGY ........................ Hollace Colburn
```

In order of appearance:
QUINCEY: Mid-twenties, pleasant, open, honest, a young writer.
PAT: Mid-thirties, tall, attractive, witty. A charming alcoholic.
ELLIE: Mid-thirties, attractive, cool. A college professor.
MARGO: Forties, a well-known writer, attractive, self-contained, super-charming.
PEGGY: Mid-thirties, a chic suburban housewife trying to do everything "right."

CAUTION: Professionals and amateurs are hereby warned that

A LATE SNOW

is subject to a royalty. The play is fully protected under the copyright laws of the United States of America, and of all countries covered by the International Copyright Union (including the Dominion of Canada and the rest of the British Commonwealth), and of all countries covered by the Pan-American Copyright Convention and the Universal Copyright Convention, and of all countries with which the United States has reciprocal copyright relations. All rights, including professional, amateur, motion picture, recitation, lecturing, public reading, classroom or workshop performance, radio broadcasting, television, and the rights of translation into foreign languages, are strictly reserved by the author. Particular emphasis is laid upon the question of readings and the use of this play for classroom, workshop or audition purposes, permission for which must be secured from the author in writing. No portion of the play may be published, reprinted in any publication, or copied for any reason without permission of the publisher.

No performances, professional or amateur, of this play may be given without obtaining the written permission of the publisher, and paying the requisite fee. All inquiries should be addressed to JH Press, P. O. Box 294, Village Station, New York, N.Y. 10014.

ACT ONE

It is late afternoon in early spring. As the curtain rises, we see the interior of a cabin by a lake.

Downstairs, a living room and a kitchen, somehow separated from one another. The living room has a fireplace, although we need not see the fire. It also has a big window overlooking the lake, which can be the "fourth wall."

The second floor, which can be indicated by risers, has two small bedrooms and a door leading to a bath. There should be steps of some kind from one level to the other, indicating a stairway.

Downstairs, there are two doors: a front door, off the living room; a back door, off the kitchen.

Furnishings are comfortable and worn. Books and artifacts are tossed comfortably around. There is a bar area in the living room and a set of wind chimes in the master bedroom window.

QUINCEY opens the door to the living room from the outside with a key.

QUINCEY: I hope you can get that truck back out of here.

PAT'S VOICE: Oh, sure. It's got four-wheel drive. Just prop the door open.

(QUINCEY *does so.*)

PAT'S VOICE: I've got the tailgate down. We can roll it in. Come on.

(QUINCEY *goes back out. We hear the sound of something heavy being moved.*)

QUINCEY'S VOICE: It weighs a ton.

PAT'S VOICE: You wouldn't listen. I tried to sell you something nice and light—an end table, a dry sink. . . .

QUINCEY'S VOICE: This is the piece she wants. She talks about it all the time.

(*They appear, pushing an antique Dutch cupboard.*)

PAT'S VOICE: Lift it over the sill.

QUINCEY: (*Looking at the heavy object*) Lift it over the sill.

PAT: Come on.

(*With a mighty effort,* QUINCEY *does so.*)

QUINCEY: Mother of God.

PAT: Good. Now we just roll it into place.

QUINCEY: It goes over there.

PAT: I know where it goes.

QUINCEY: Watch the rug.

PAT: Push!

QUINCEY: Don't scratch it!

PAT: Just push, will you?

QUINCEY: Don't scrape the floor!

PAT: You're really uptight, aren't you? (*She pushes the piece into place, scraping the floor.*)

QUINCEY: You scraped the floor! (*She looks closely.*) Shit.

PAT: Spit on it. (QUINCEY *looks at her, puzzled.*) Spit on it and rub it with your finger.

QUINCEY: (*Does so.*) It's a gouge.

PAT: It's a scratch. She'll never notice. You can't hurt these floors. (QUINCEY *continues to spit and rub.*) What does she do, beat you?

QUINCEY: I'm not even supposed to be out here. I mean, she's never said, "Here are the keys, go out to the cabin."

PAT: Aren't you here every weekend?

QUINCEY: With Ellie. After all, it's her house.

PAT: It's her house. (*She looks around.*) It looks the same. I miss it. (*Quickly*) I never did like that piece. It's junk.

QUINCEY: Why did you take it?

PAT: Because Ellie wanted it. I figured some sucker would buy it.

QUINCEY: Ellie says you took half the stuff in the place.

PAT: Well, half of it was mine. She took the lamp. I wanted that. (*She indicates a Tiffany shade.*) That's worth something—a couple of hundred.

QUINCEY: Don't touch that!

PAT: Just looking.

QUINCEY: (*About scratch*) I hope she won't notice.

PAT: She will.

QUINCEY: You said she wouldn't!

PAT: (*Smiles*) I lied. (*She examines shade closely.*) If I put this in the shop tomorrow morning, it'd be sold by noon. Three hundred, easy.

QUINCEY: Come on, don't touch that!

PAT: Red glass is rare. Do you know why?

QUINCEY: Leave it alone!

PAT: They use gold to make red glass. Gold.

QUINCEY: Please. I never should have brought you out here.

PAT: You wanted delivery. You drove a hard bargain.

QUINCEY: Bullshit. I paid you twice what that piece is worth.

PAT: That's true. Actually, you paid much more than twice. Ellie and I found that piece of junk in an abandoned barn, four years ago.

QUINCEY: (*Defensively*) She loves it. She's always saying, "I wish I had my old cupboard." She kept her papers in it, I think.

PAT: Her private treasure chest. I used to love to go through it when she was out of the house. She kept little notebooks. . . .

QUINCEY: She still does. She has an old library table in the apartment. She keeps her notebooks in the drawer.

PAT: "Pat drunk seventeen days this month. Rash on my right hand getting worse. Psychological? Order a cord of wood by the thirtieth." A veritable font of information, huh?

QUINCEY: I don't know. I never look.

PAT: You should. Ellie rarely tells you what she's really thinking. "Pat's stories too pat. Something's going on."

QUINCEY: I shouldn't have brought you out here.

PAT: I still have keys.

QUINCEY: She changed the lock.

PAT: She take a Peace Bond out on me, too?

QUINCEY: Ellie says you'd steal the gold from your grandmother's teeth.

PAT: (*Grins.*) There's a lot of stuff here I'd like to have.

QUINCEY: It belongs to Ellie.

PAT: It belongs to both of us.

QUINCEY: Not any more.

PAT: Where'd you get those keys?

QUINCEY: I took them out of her bureau drawer.

PAT: Before you establish your territorial prerogative, you'd better get your own keys. (*She goes to bar.*) Want a drink?

QUINCEY: We can't stay.

PAT: Why'd you come to my shop?

QUINCEY: To buy that cupboard.

PAT: Really?

QUINCEY: It's our anniversary. Our first anniversary. I want to give her something special.

PAT: When is it?—your anniversary? What's the date?

QUINCEY: The eighteenth.

PAT: Amazing. Sure you won't join me? (*She continues to case the house as she drinks.*)

QUINCEY: We've got to go.

PAT: No hurry. I've closed shop for the day.

QUINCEY: We shouldn't stay out here.

PAT: The eighteenth of April. Ours was June twenty-fourth. It wasn't really, but I convinced Ellie it was—it was close enough. All my anniversaries are June twenty-fourth. It's the only way I can remember: 6-24—the first three digits of my social security. (*She picks up an object.*)

QUINCEY: Come on. Don't.

PAT: Why'd you come to my shop?

QUINCEY: (*Taking object from her*) It was the only way to get the cupboard.

PAT: There are a couple of cupboards just like that every weekend at the flea market.

QUINCEY: That cupboard is special.

PAT: It looks like all the others. She wouldn't know the difference. . . . You've walked by before. I've seen you.

QUINCEY: You lived with her for five years. You were an important part of her life.

PAT: (*Satisfied*) I never should have let her buy me out.

QUINCEY: You made her buy you out!

PAT: She wouldn't let me live here and I needed the money.

QUINCEY: She didn't have it.

PAT: She got it though. She could always get money if she had to. The pleasures of a Good Credit rating. (*Pause*) We laid these floors ourselves—and framed the windows—

QUINCEY: We've got to go now.

PAT: Ellie's mother sent us those drapes.

QUINCEY: It'll be dark soon.

PAT: So what? You said she won't be back until Sunday.

QUINCEY: The conference isn't over until Saturday night. She's flying back on Sunday.

PAT: When we bought this place there was no insulation, no paneling, you could see the ground through the floorboards.

QUINCEY: Please, Pat, let's go.

PAT: She's really got you tied up, hasn't she? Little Miss Step and Fetch It. Ellie loves to give orders. I never took them. (*She goes back to bar.*) Are you a teetotaler, too?

QUINCEY: No. Are you going to be able to drive?

PAT: My reputation precedes me.

QUINCEY: Ellie says you have a problem.

PAT: (*Pours them each a drink.*) Ellie says I'm a drunk. She's at a conference?

QUINCEY: In Philadelphia. University department heads.

PAT: She go alone?

QUINCEY: With the other university department heads.

PAT: I never knew a conference to end on a Saturday night. (*She hands* QUINCEY *a drink.*) Cheers. (*At window*) When did the ice go this year?

QUINCEY: Sometime last week, I think.

PAT: We used to bet on the day.

QUINCEY: We weren't out here.

PAT: Ever see it go?

QUINCEY: No.

PAT: It starts melting around the edges. For a few days, it's slush for maybe fifteen, twenty feet around the shoreline. Then the circle of ice that's left in the middle of the lake gets gray, then black—then WHOOSH. It goes under in ten seconds. The black lake turns navy, then sky blue. And it's spring. (*She surveys the cabin.*) You a student of Ellie's?

QUINCEY: I was—last year when I was in grad school. I'm a writer.

PAT: Published?

QUINCEY: No.

PAT: How do you earn a living?

QUINCEY: I edit a throwaway.

PAT: What?

QUINCEY: One of those four-page weekly papers with neighborhood news and a lot of ads that you find in your mailbox.

PAT: I didn't know Ellie was into seducing her students.

QUINCEY: She's not. I pursued her. It wasn't easy. She wasn't over you.

PAT: Oh?

QUINCEY: I lived with your ghost for months.

PAT: She never answered my letters. She hung up when I called her.

QUINCEY: Five years is a long time.

PAT: Yes, it is.

QUINCEY: It takes a while to get over it. She's over it now.

PAT: Chilly in here. Let's start a fire.

QUINCEY: Let's go.

PAT: There's wood in the crib by the fireplace. You know how to start a fire?

QUINCEY: Of course.

PAT: Well, do it. I'm going to take a look upstairs.

QUINCEY: No.

PAT: (*Charming*) She'll never know.

QUINCEY: No.

PAT: For old times' sake.

QUINCEY: No.

PAT: (*Handing her the starter wood*) Placate me. Lonely, nearing middle age, with a slight tendency to imbibe, a pitiful figure . . . (QUINCEY *laughs in spite of herself.*) Good girl.

QUINCEY: Don't take anything!

PAT: (*Going upstairs*) You can frisk me when I come down.

(QUINCEY *begins to make a fire. We hear a car motor, see lights flash across the kitchen.* QUINCEY *looks up quizzically as the key turns in the back door.*

ELLIE *enters.*)

QUINCEY: Oh, shit.

ELLIE: Quincey!

QUINCEY: You're back early!

(QUINCEY *embraces* ELLIE, *who responds perfunctorily, then pulls nervously away.* ELLIE *is dismayed by* QUINCEY's *unexpected presence but tries valiantly not to show it.*)

QUINCEY: I wanted to surprise you!

ELLIE: You did.

(QUINCEY *pulls* ELLIE *to the cupboard.*)

QUINCEY: With this. (*She hugs* ELLIE.) Happy First Anniversary!

ELLIE: Quincey, where did you get this?

(*At the back door,* MARGO *appears, suitcase in hand. She stands there, unnoticed.*)

QUINCEY: (*About the cupboard*) Surprise!

ELLIE: Where did you get it?

QUINCEY: It's what you wanted!

ELLIE: It's just like the old one.

QUINCEY: It *is* the old one.

MARGO: May I come in?

(ELLIE *looks from* MARGO *to* QUINCEY, *back to* MARGO. *She is flustered.*)

QUINCEY: Hello.

MARGO: Hello.

ELLIE: (*Recovering*) This is Quincey Evans, a former student of mine. Quincey, Margo Bettis.

QUINCEY: Margo. *The* Margo Bettis?

MARGO: The only one I know.

QUINCEY: *A Memory of Autumn, The Last Question, Miller's Breach, Afternoon in* . . .

MARGO: Amazing.

QUINCEY: I took a course in you. Ellie teaches a course in you.

MARGO: I know. Margot Bettis a multiple-choice answer.

QUINCEY: You're always an essay. I thought you were retired (*Catches herself.*)—a recluse. I thought you never came out in public.

MARGO: Only after dark.

QUINCEY: I mean, you never give interviews, or . . . (*Shrugs.*) I'm getting in deeper, aren't I? Sorry. Welcome. (*To* ELLIE) Where did you find her?

ELLIE: Margo was the guest lecturer at the conference. We flew back together.

MARGO: She's trying to coerce me into teaching.

ELLIE: A lecture series. Wouldn't that be a coup?

QUINCEY: Terrific. You're a kind of cult among the undergrads.

MARGO: It terrifies me.

QUINCEY: I have everything you've ever written.

ELLIE: I asked Margo to spend the day here tomorrow—so I can do my sales pitch.

QUINCEY: It's like seeing a legend come to life.

ELLIE: I promised her a quiet day by the lake.

QUINCEY: I hope we'll have time to talk. I have a thousand questions.

ELLIE: I have yet to sell her on the joys of university life.

QUINCEY: I'm a writer, too, you know. Fledgling but good, I think.

MARGO: Ellie, I'm tired . . . and a little uncomfortable. Can I change?

ELLIE: Of course. Upstairs. Excuse us, Quincey.

(ELLIE *picks up* MARGO's *bag, starts up the stairs. She encounters* PAT *on her way down.* ELLIE *is startled and angry at* PAT's *presence.*)

PAT: Hi.

ELLIE: What are you doing here?

PAT: I came with the cupboard.

QUINCEY: She insisted: free delivery.

PAT: (*To* ELLIE) Thank you?

ELLIE: Thank you. Excuse us, please.

(*She leads* MARGO, *bewildered, upstairs.* MARGO *stops at the master bedroom.*

MARGO: What a cozy room. And a beautiful view of the lake.

ELLIE: Yes. (*Pause.*) Put your things anywhere.

MARGO: But this is your room, isn't it?

ELLIE: It's the nicest room. The guest room is kind of sparse. I'll sleep there.

MARGO: No.

ELLIE: Please. I insist.

MARGO: No. It's your room.

ELLIE: The guest room overlooks the compost heap. Please?

MARGO: All right.

ELLIE: It's the least I can do. (*Pause.*) I'm sorry. I didn't expect anyone to be here.

MARGO: (*Smiles.*) It's a regular party, isn't it?

ELLIE: They'll be leaving soon.

MARGO: It's all right.

ELLIE: It's not all right. I promised you a quiet weekend.

MARGO: They're your friends. I'm sure they're interesting people. (*She starts to undress.*) Aren't they?

ELLIE: (*Ignoring that*) I know how you feel about meeting strangers.

MARGO: That's my problem. I'm a big girl now. I can take care of myself.

ELLIE: I'm sorry about Quincey. She's young and exuberant. She didn't mean to embarrass you.

MARGO: Embarrass me? I was flattered. Would you hand me that shirt, please?

(*Downstairs.*)

PAT: (*To* QUINCEY) Well, well. Aren't you glad we stuck around?

QUINCEY: Cool it. That's business.

PAT: I'll say.

QUINCEY: Don't you know who she is?

PAT: I heard your eulogy.

QUINCEY: She's like a myth. I've never seen a picture of her. I've read everything she's ever written, but I never knew what she looked like before.

PAT: You won't forget.

QUINCEY: Ellie has many business associates. That's what this is. I know Ellie.

PAT: I guess I don't. I thought she was true-blue-lou.

QUINCEY: She is.

(*Upstairs,* ELLIE *is uncomfortable watching* MARGO.)

ELLIE: They won't stay long.

MARGO: Will you stop worrying?

ELLIE: Sorry. I'll go downstairs and take care of it. (*Pause.*) Are you all right?

MARGO: I'm fine. Just fine.

(ELLIE *descends the stairs as* PAT *is pouring another drink.*)

ELLIE: Quincey? Thank you. (*She hugs* QUINCEY *warmly*.) I'm sorry I was abrupt—I was just stunned to find you here.

QUINCEY: It's all right.

ELLIE: It was an opportunity that I couldn't pass up, honey. Every university in the country has tried to get Margo on faculty. No one's ever succeeded. We seemed to hit it off at the conference. . . . Honey, she doesn't know. . . . I mean, I haven't said anything. So, play it cool?

QUINCEY: I hate doing that.

ELLIE: Please?

QUINCEY: It's important to you, isn't it?

PAT: (*Entering their area*) So, how are you, Ellie?

ELLIE: Fine, Pat. And you?

PAT: Fine.

ELLIE: Good.

PAT: You look well.

ELLIE: So do you.

PAT: The house looks good.

ELLIE: It's a nice house.

PAT: It always was, I miss it.

ELLIE: It's been good seeing you, Pat. I appreciate your bringing the cupboard out. You don't mind giving Quincey a ride back to town, do you?

PAT: (*Pause.*) I see.

ELLIE: I have work to do.

QUINCEY: I'd like to stay, Ellie. I'd like to talk to her.

ELLIE: If I get her to sign a contract, you'll have lots of chances to talk to her. (*Pause.*) It wouldn't look good, honey. I'm sorry, Quincey.

(PAT *grins.* MARGO *comes down the stairs, sloppy, comfortable.*)

MARGO: This is the real person. That other lady is a sham.

PAT: Hi.

ELLIE: Oh. Margo, this is Pat Leonard.

PAT: I've read your work.

MARGO: And?

PAT: You're good.

QUINCEY: Great.

MARGO: You really are a fan, aren't you?

QUINCEY: An admirer. Fan sounds—childish.

PAT: You must be used to adulation.

MARGO: Not at all. I don't see many people. That's one of the things that distresses me about Ellie's idea.

QUINCEY: Lecturing.

MARGO: It terrifies me. All those people!

QUINCEY: Adoring you.

MARGO: Why? For what?

QUINCEY: For being one of the best writers in the world.

MARGO: She's tenacious.

PAT: Ellie can testify to that.

ELLIE: I don't know what you're talking about.

PAT: Quincey told me about your first meeting.

MARGO: Oh? (*Pause.*) Well?

QUINCEY: It's not a very interesting story. I want to talk to you. If I could have picked any writer in the world to interview, it would have been you: and here you are.

MARGO: I'm overwhelmed. I'm also hungry. How about some supper?

ELLIE: Pat and Quincey have to get back to town.

MARGO: We bought plenty of food—Ellie and I stopped in this marvelous little country store. . . .

PAT: O'Brien's.

MARGO: You know it?

PAT: Well.

MARGO: And I'm cooking.

ELLIE: No.

MARGO: Yes. Does that tempt you?

QUINCEY: Ellie . . .

PAT: We'd love to stay.

MARGO: Good!

QUINCEY: We'll leave right after supper.

MARGO: You (*To* ELLIE) go upstairs and change. Get comfortable. You two (*To* PAT *and* QUINCEY) bring in the groceries. (ELLIE, *reluctantly, starts for stairs.*) Go on! (PAT *grins and goes for the groceries.* QUINCEY *tries to elicit some response from* ELLIE, *but* ELLIE *goes upstairs. To* QUINCEY) I neglected to mention that I haven't cooked since Thanksgiving three years ago when my sister was having her fifth baby.

QUINCEY: How do you eat?

MARGO: I live in a hotel. There's a restaurant downstairs.

QUINCEY: That must be expensive.

MARGO: Money buys time. And time is something a writer never has enough of. You'll find that out.

QUINCEY: You live alone?

MARGO: Yes.

QUINCEY: I don't think I'll ever want to live alone.

MARGO: You never have?

QUINCEY: No. My family, then college, then—roommates.

MARGO: You should try it alone. Everyone should. Builds an independent person.

QUINCEY: I always want to have a lover.

MARGO: Just don't get married and have babies. It drains your creative juices.

QUINCEY: That isn't exactly what I had in mind.

MARGO: You have a boyfriend?

QUINCEY: Well, I have had a boyfriend. A lot of them, as a matter of fact.

MARGO: I should think so. You're a nice-looking girl.

(PAT *enters with groceries.*)

PAT: You're not doing your share, Quincey, friend.

QUINCEY: Oh. Sorry. I'll get the rest.

PAT: That's it.

MARGO: Don't stand there like Samson. Those must be heavy. Put them down. (PAT *does.*) I hope there's no one here with a weight problem. (*She takes spaghetti out of the bag.*) We're having spaghetti. Fan—admirer—want to help?

QUINCEY: Sure.

PAT: You never got that fire going, did you?

(*Without waiting for an answer,* PAT *heads to the fireplace.*

ELLIE *comes down the stairs.*)

ELLIE: (*To kitchen*) Everything under control?

MARGO: Fine. The fan—

QUINCEY: Admirer.

MARGO: —is helping.

ELLIE: What can I do?

MARGO: Nothing. Out of the kitchen! Too many cooks . . .

ELLIE: You're sure? If you need me . . .

(*As* ELLIE *enters living room:*)

PAT: I need you. Give me some newspapers off that pile.

ELLIE: (*Doing so*) You always had a talent for that.

PAT: You haven't had a fire since.

ELLIE: Don't flatter yourself. I've managed.

PAT: You still think I'm a scoundrel, don't you?

ELLIE: Aren't you?

PAT: I never thought so.

ELLIE: Pat, I don't want to get into that.

PAT: I didn't mean to be.

ELLIE: It's over, let's forget it. Okay?

PAT: It's not over. The ice sank last week.

ELLIE: I didn't see it.

PAT: It's going to be spring.

ELLIE: It looks like snow to me.

PAT: All dead things come to life.

ELLIE: No. It looks like snow.

PAT: I'm sorry. You never gave me a chance to say I'm sorry. You wouldn't see me, talk to me. You never gave us a chance.

ELLIE: (*Pause.*) Did you give Cassie a chance?

PAT: I never loved her.

ELLIE: You made love to her—drunk. You wrapped her in a car around a walnut tree and you walked away.

PAT: It was an accident.

ELLIE: She was my friend.

PAT: You hated her.

ELLIE: I hated her for having for affair with you, for making a fool out of me, for lying to me. For loving you.

PAT: It didn't mean anything, Ellie. It never meant anything.

ELLIE: Cassie's dead, Pat. That means something.

PAT: It was an accident.

ELLIE: Everything's an accident. It's an accident you drink too much. It's an accident you fall into bed with the nearest available woman. It's an accident that they all fall in love with you, even when you don't want them. Cassie is dead and you say, it was an accident.

PAT: Don't you think I feel anything?

ELLIE: I don't know.

PAT: I didn't want to kill anybody. I never wanted to hurt anybody. I'm sorry Cassie's dead. I'm sorry, sorry, sorry, I've said it a million times, asleep and awake. I know there's no price on a human life but I've paid, Ellie, I've paid. The court wiped out my trust fund; my father, the compassionate bastard, wiped me out of his will. I lost my home, I nearly lost my business. And I lost you.

ELLIE: I was just someone to come home to between binges, between affairs. Not much of a loss, Pat.

PAT: I loved you.

ELLIE: (*Pause.*) I loved you.

PAT: What happened to us?

ELLIE: Maybe five years is too long.

PAT: I wanted to be with you for a lifetime. I had a dream: two crochety old ladies rocking on that front porch, waiting for the ice to go. (*Pause*.) She's not enough for you, Ellie. You need more than that.

ELLIE: She's bright and honest—and she loves me.

PAT: She's there when you come home. Faithful and comfortable. Only a year and you're bored to death.

ELLIE: That's not true.

PAT: Then why the house guest?

ELLIE: The house guest is here on business. I don't know anything about her—personal preferences.

PAT: But you've got a feeling, haven't you?

(QUINCEY *enters the living room.*)

QUINCEY: Ellie, do we have a garlic press?

PAT: (*Smartly*) Bottom drawer on the left, under the sink.

QUINCEY: Ellie?

ELLIE: That's right.

(QUINCEY *exits.*)

PAT: Little Miss Step and Fetch It. But cute. I'll admit that. Cute.

ELLIE: You're jealous.

PAT: Not of her.

ELLIE: She's good for me.

PAT: She worships you. Good for your ego.

ELLIE: You won't give up, will you?

PAT: She's no challenge. That's what makes the knees tremble and the wind chimes ring: the challenge. Without it, boredom.

ELLIE: If challenge means sitting up night after night wondering in whose bed you'll find your drunken lover, I've had enough challenge for a lifetime, thanks.

(*From the kitchen,* MARGO's *voice.*)

MARGO: All right, you two. I need some help!

PAT: (*To* ELLIE) Obviously, you haven't. (*To* MARGO) Coming!

(*They go into the kitchen.*)

MARGO: (*To* ELLIE) I understand you make magnificent sauce.

PAT: She does.

MARGO: (*To* PAT) And what are you good at?

PAT: (*Grinning*) My specialty is—mixing drinks.

ELLIE: (*Warning*) Pat . . .

MARGO: Mine is drinking them. (*To* ELLIE, *about the kitchen*) It's all yours. Let me know when you're ready for the spaghetti to go in.

(PAT *and* MARGO *go into the living room,* ELLIE *looking worriedly after them.*)

QUINCEY: (*To* ELLIE) Hi. I love you. I missed you.

(ELLIE *smiles nervously, proceeds to make sauce.* QUINCEY *presses garlic, cuts bread, etc.*

In the living room:)

MARGO: Straight up. A shot glass is fine.

PAT: I can tell you're my kind of woman.

(*In the kitchen:*)

QUINCEY: I'm jealous.

ELLIE: Don't be silly. I don't even know the woman.

QUINCEY: Not her. Pat.

ELLIE: I was crazy for five years. I won't go back.

QUINCEY: Sometimes I think you're still in love with her.

ELLIE: (*Ignoring that*) She's getting drunk, Quincey. You've got to get her out of here right after supper. Can you drive that truck of hers?

QUINCEY: I suppose so.

ELLIE: She's uncontrollable when she's drunk. She talks too much.

QUINCEY: That could be embarrassing.

ELLIE: And she'll try to seduce anyone—if she thinks it'll hurt me.

QUINCEY: Don't worry. I wouldn't fall for that.

   (*In the living room:*)

MARGO: (*At window*) It looks like snow.

PAT: No way. It's too late in the season.

MARGO: It's a snow sky. (*She accepts drink.*) Thank you. So, exactly who are you?

PAT: (*Looking at sky*) A friend.

MARGO: Oh?

PAT: An ex-friend.

MARGO: You don't know which?

PAT: Like the weather up here, it could change any minute.

MARGO: You're from this area?

PAT: I lived here for five years. In this house.

MARGO: Oh. Ellie bought it from you?

PAT: Partly.

MARGO: What do you do?

PAT: I restore old things. Antiques.

MARGO: How about old writers?

PAT: I could open a department. (*Pause.*) You're not old.

MARGO: No? I had my success so early. I peaked at twenty-five—and there are too many years left after that. Girl Genius goes dry.

PAT: You're still writing.

MARGO: Trying. Strange. I had so much to say when I was twenty-five.

PAT: Does a writer write from imagination or experience?

MARGO: Experience first. That triggers the imagination.

PAT: And you're short on experience?

MARGO: (*Pause.*) Interesting.

PAT: Are you?

MARGO: Yes. Ten years ago I closed the door. I'd had as much experience as I could bear. Enough to last, I thought. (PAT *pours another drink, looks questioningly at* MARGO.) Not yet. But meeting Ellie this week . . .

PAT: Yes?

MARGO: So full of life, of ideas. I never thought of teaching.

PAT: Ellie loves it.

MARGO: It frightens me.

PAT: It's a challenge.

MARGO: Ellie makes me feel that I can do it. She makes me feel alive again—brave.

PAT: I see.

MARGO: (*Quickly, to kitchen*) How are you doing in there?

(*From kitchen:*)

ELLIE: Under way. (*To* QUINCEY) Go in the living room, honey. Relax.

QUINCEY: I'd rather stay with you.

ELLIE: I'd rather you kept an eye on Pat.

QUINCEY: (*Reluctantly*) Oh. (*She gives* ELLIE *a kiss as she goes into the living room.* ELLIE *gives her a warning look.*) Sorry. Just doing what comes naturally. (*She goes into the living room.*)

MARGO: Whatever it is, it smells good.

QUINCEY: It'll be good. Ellie's a super cook.

PAT: (*To* QUINCEY) You think everybody's just wonderful, don't you?

QUINCEY: (*To* PAT) Not necessarily.

MARGO: (*Quickly*) I'm sure Ellie cooks as well as she does everything else.

PAT: We're obviously all aware of Ellie's talents.

QUINCEY: (*Confused, quickly*) Tell me about the conference.

MARGO: The conference?

QUINCEY: In Philadelphia.

MARGO: Oh. Well, I gave a timid little lecture and Ellie led the applause.

QUINCEY: Where did you stay?

MARGO: The Concord.

QUINCEY: So did Ellie.

MARGO: Yes. Everyone at the conference stayed at the Concord. It's a lovely old hotel.

QUINCEY: I've never been there. I've never been to a conference.

PAT: You haven't missed a thing.

MARGO: You meet, have assemblies, lectures. . . .

QUINCEY: Day and night?

MARGO: Days mostly. There was a terrible dinner the first night—a command performance. Shoeleather steaks, frozen vegetables and speakers. Deadly. Everyone glued themselves to the bar afterward, I'm told. The turnout at the early session the next morning must have been very small.

QUINCEY: Ellie doesn't drink.

MARGO: We didn't stay. We spent the evening talking.

QUINCEY: In your room?

MARGO: In hers. (*To* PAT) Would you freshen this?

QUINCEY: Me, too.

PAT: (*To* QUINCEY) Oh. Sorry. (*She starts to mix drink.*) We need ice. I'll get it. (*She goes to kitchen.*)

ELLIE: (*To* PAT) Will you take it easy?

PAT: Nag, nag. I'm just being the genial host.

ELLIE: —ess.

PAT: (*Prissy*) Hostess.

ELLIE: The trouble with you is you don't like women.

PAT: Are you kidding?

ELLIE: You don't. Not really. You don't like yourself and you don't like other women.

PAT: Stop philosophizing and keep cooking. (*She slaps* ELLIE *on the ass and exits to living room with ice.*)

MARGO: I know that I'd enjoy working with Ellie.

PAT: (*Entering*) Ice, coming up.

(*In the kitchen,* ELLIE *tosses her apron on the sink and heads to the living room.*)

MARGO: But I'm nervous about making a commitment—to teaching.

ELLIE: (*Entering*) The sauce is simmering. You can put on the water for the spaghetti.

MARGO: (*Charmingly to* QUINCEY) Would you?

ELLIE: (*Before* QUINCEY *can answer*) Thanks, honey.

(QUINCEY, *irritated, goes to kitchen.*)

PAT: We were having a fascinating conversation: how you and Margo discovered one another across a crowded room in Philadelphia.

MARGO: That's not quite what I said.

PAT: And changed the course of one another's lives.

ELLIE: Pat!

MARGO: Of my life. I said that meeting you was meaningful to me. (*An awkward pause.*) And it might well change the course of my life. (*Laughs.*) It's a course that could use some changing, believe me.

PAT: (*To* ELLIE) Your boundless enthusiasm and zest for challenge has sparked new life, presented new horizons.

ELLIE: I've always admired Margo's work.

PAT: Presto! A marriage—of talents.

ELLIE: Will you shut up?

(MARGO *and* ELLIE *smile at each other.*)

PAT: (*In frustration*) Where's the poker. I want to stoke the fire.

ELLIE: (*Crossing to the window*) I don't know. In the crib. Look for it.

MARGO: Pat used to live here, she was telling me.

ELLIE: She was?

PAT: We used to live here together.

MARGO: I thought perhaps something like that. (ELLIE *looks at her quickly.*) You're snippy with each other. You must know each other very well.

PAT: Perceptive.

MARGO: It goes with being a writer. Occupational handicap—or advantage. Depends on your point of view.

PAT: She lives with Quincey now.

 (ELLIE *looks sharply at* PAT.)

MARGO: Oh.

ELLIE: (*Quickly*) We share an apartment near the university. Rents are very high.

MARGO: And you. Do you have a roommate, Pat?

PAT: Sometimes. And sometimes not.

MARGO: I guess I'm the only loner here. I have had roommates though. (ELLIE *and* PAT *look with interest.*) I remember my college roommate. (*She laughs.*)

PAT: I never had a college roommate. Ellie did.

MARGO: Mine had peroxide hair. Frizzy. She lost her virginity in the entrance hall, after hours, her freshman year. Bled all over the bathroom. Put me in a state of terror: I was sure that going to bed with a man was tantamount to a seige of battle.

PAT: Wasn't it?

(MARGO *just smiles.*)

ELLIE: My college roommate was beautiful. The most beautiful girl on campus. The jocks used to line up in the lounge, waiting for her. She gave them all a hard time.

PAT: Perfect Peggy. (*To* MARGO) You'll excuse my attitude but I've heard this story a thousand times.

MARGO: You're about to hear it again. I'm interested.

ELLIE: No. (*Pause.*) She was just perfect, that's all.

MARGO: (*Easily*) And you loved her.

ELLIE: (*Taken aback*) Yes.

MARGO: It's nice to remember friends we've loved. What happened to her?

PAT: Perfect Peggy panicked. She got married.

MARGO: That's nice. Do you hear from her?

ELLIE: Christmas cards, now and then.

MARGO: You should look her up. It's fun to see how people change.

ELLIE: I'd rather remember her.

PAT: You can control your memories. You don't have to remember that she had a large wart on the back of her ear. . . .

ELLIE: She didn't have any warts!

PAT: Or she picked her nose.

ELLIE: Pat!

PAT: Or she drank a little too much. (*She pours herself another drink.*)

ELLIE: Stop it.

PAT: Or she fooled around. . . . (*She offers* MARGO *a drink.* MARGO *refuses.*) You can shine memories up real nice. But live people—they're a little harder to control.

ELLIE: (*Quickly*) I wrote to her recently, as a matter of fact. I told her about the cabin and invited her to bring her family up some weekend.

PAT: No kidding?

ELLIE: I don't know why I did that. I was—

PAT: Bored. (ELLIE *looks sharply at* PAT.) I'd like to meet Perfect Peggy.

ELLIE: I hope that can be avoided. (QUINCEY *enters, pours another drink.*) How's it going, Quincey? (QUINCEY *doesn't respond.*) Take it easy. You're not a drinker. (QUINCEY *slugs it.*) Are you all right?

QUINCEY: I think I'm not going to feel so good.

ELLIE: Go upstairs and lie down.

QUINCEY: Not on your life.

MARGO: We were talking about college roommates. Did you have a college roommate, Quincey?

PAT: Yeah. The professor.

QUINCEY: I only lived in the dorm six months. It wasn't my style. I couldn't feel free there. It's an up-tight school. (*To* ELLIE) Sorry, it's true.

MARGO: What do you mean, "up-tight"?

PAT: It means closed up tight, constipated.

ELLIE: Pat!

MARGO: I know what the word means. I haven't been dead—just cloistered.

QUINCEY: For instance: (*A pause. She doesn't know whether to go ahead or not.*) One person, a sophomore, tried to form a Gay Lib group. . . .

MARGO: Gay Lib? (*To* PAT) I know what it means.

PAT: I figured you did.

MARGO: (*To* QUINCEY) And?

QUINCEY: They kicked her out of the dorm.

MARGO: Who did?

QUINCEY: The administration. The rest of the kids, we rallied and picketed and the trustees had a hearing. They let her stay in school—

if she lived off campus. She couldn't live in the dorm.

ELLIE: Quincey . . .

QUINCEY: It's true, isn't it?

ELLIE: It was four years ago. The administration has changed. There are some radical groups on campus now.

QUINCEY: The faculty's still in the closet.

MARGO: Ellie tells me there's a professed Communist on the staff. That's a far cry from my college days.

QUINCEY: There may be a two-headed donkey, too, but there sure as hell aren't any homosexuals!

ELLIE: It's a conservative school. This is a conservative state.

QUINCEY: Somebody has to make change happen. Somebody who believes in the goodness of themselves, of what they are.

PAT: So do it.

QUINCEY: (*Frantically*) I can't. I want to be honest and free and proud . . . Everything I do reflects on Ellie.

ELLIE: Quincey, that's enough. (QUINCEY *turns and runs upstairs to the bedroom.*) She's not used to drinking.

MARGO: She seems to be really upset.

ELLIE: I'll go. (*Follows* QUINCEY *upstairs.*)

MARGO: (*To* PAT) Well. I'm not sure I know what all that was about.

PAT: I expect you do.

MARGO: Young people are all crusaders these days.

PAT: Come on, Margo. Don't give me that "Lawsy, Miss Scarlett, I don't know nothing about birthing babies" act.

MARGO: I don't know what you're talking about. (*Rises.*) I'd better check on the spaghetti. I hope Quincey will feel like eating. I made enough for six people. (*She passes the window.*) See? I told you it looked like snow.

PAT: (*Looking out window*) Well, I'll be damned.

(MARGO *goes to kitchen, leaving* PAT *in living room.* PAT *pours another drink. Upstairs:*)

ELLIE: Quincey . . .

QUINCEY: Why'd you put her in our room?

ELLIE: It's the nicest room. She's a special guest.

QUINCEY: You really want to impress her, don't you?

ELLIE: I did.

QUINCEY: I'm sorry. I couldn't help it. I didn't say anything about you.

ELLIE: If she doesn't know, she's retarded.

QUINCEY: What difference does it make? She may be, herself. If she's not, so what? I love you. I want the world to know it.

ELLIE: I could lose my job.

QUINCEY: Oh, Ellie.

ELLIE: It makes people uncomfortable. They don't understand.

QUINCEY: It's time we made them understand.

ELLIE: Quincey, I know you're right.

QUINCEY: Then, why won't you do something about it? Aren't you proud? Don't you like yourself?

ELLIE: I like being a woman.

QUINCEY: A woman who loves other women.

ELLIE: Quincey, listen to me! When I was your age, "lesbian" was a dictionary word used only to frighten teen-age girls and parents. Mothers fainted, fathers became violent, landlords evicted you, and nobody would hire you. A lesbian was like a vampire: she looked in the mirror and there was no reflection.

QUINCEY: You're scared.

ELLIE: Of course I'm scared. I don't want to be different. I don't want people pointing fingers at me, misguided altruists feeling sorry for me.

QUINCEY: You're a VIP on campus. You could be a figurehead.

ELLIE: I don't have the courage to be a figurehead, Quincey. I'm sorry. (*She starts to leave.*)

QUINCEY: Ellie? I hope I didn't screw things up for you. I don't want to hurt you. I love you. I love you, love you, love you. (ELLIE *holds her.*) It's just that I'm so fucking tired of living in a closet!

ELLIE: (*Pause.*) Are you going to be all right?

QUINCEY: As long as I'm here.

ELLIE: Think you can come downstairs?

QUINCEY: Give me a minute. (ELLIE *releases her, starts to leave.*) I'm sorry.

ELLIE: So am I.

QUINCEY: Someday.

ELLIE: I hope so. (*She comes down the stairs, into the kitchen. To* MARGO) She's all right. Just a little too much to drink. She'll be down for supper.

MARGO: Good.

ELLIE: Can I help?

MARGO: In a minute.

(ELLIE *goes into living room.*)

ELLIE: It's snowing.

PAT: Hard and fast. So I was wrong. I'm not often wrong.

ELLIE: You'd better go right after supper, Pat. I don't want you marooned here all night.

PAT: Don't worry. I've got four-wheel drive. Is the kid all right?

ELLIE: She's not a kid.

PAT: Sorry. Is the young woman all right?

ELLIE: She'll be fine. She doesn't have your tolerance for alcohol.

PAT: She doesn't have my experience.

ELLIE: Thank God.

PAT: You're not in love with her.

ELLIE: I love her.

PAT: It's not the same thing.

ELLIE: It's a lot more reliable.

PAT: What are you going to do, bounce her off your knee when you hear the wind chimes again? Dump her?

ELLIE: No. I'm not going to hurt her.

PAT: You won't be able to help yourself. (*Pause.*) I'd rather you stay with Quincey.

ELLIE: What?

PAT: I'll still have a chance then.

ELLIE: Stop it.

PAT: That one (*Indicating kitchen*) is real competition. I don't want to see that happen.

ELLIE: You don't have anything to do with it.

PAT: Don't I?

(*From the kitchen:*)

MARGO: Okay, set the table!

(ELLIE *begins to do so,* PAT *pours another drink in the living room.* QUINCEY *comes down the stairs,* PAT *sees her, motions her in.*)

PAT: How're you feeling?

QUINCEY: Better.

PAT: This stuff is poison. You got to work up a tolerance, takes years.

QUINCEY: You ought to know.

PAT: What are you going to do?

QUINCEY: About what?

PAT: Your celebrity rival in there.

QUINCEY: She's no rival.

PAT: I wouldn't jump to that conclusion.

QUINCEY: Ellie says you're a troublemaker.

PAT: Do you believe everything Ellie says?

QUINCEY: Most of it. She's as honest as she can be. She wouldn't hurt me.

PAT: She wouldn't mean to. (*Pause.*) I know a game that will nip that in the bud.

QUINCEY: No games. I don't play games.

PAT: It's your funeral.

QUINCEY: (*Pause.*) What is the game?

PAT: I'll come on to you, see. She'll get jealous . . .

QUINCEY: No.

PAT: It'll work.

QUINCEY: No.

PAT: Couldn't hurt.

QUINCEY: No. I won't play games with Ellie.

(ELLIE *enters.*)

PAT: We're getting to know each other.

ELLIE: How about earning your supper?

QUINCEY: I'll get the flatware.

PAT: Want another drink first, Quincey?

ELLIE: She's had enough.

PAT: Oh, listen to Mommy.

QUINCEY: I don't want another drink.

ELLIE: (*At window*) It's really coming down.

(PAT *is at bar.*)

PAT: A late snow. Something like a last chance, wouldn't you say?

(MARGO *enters.*)

MARGO: What was that?

PAT: A late snow. Something like a last chance.

MARGO: (*Pause.*) I suppose so.

(*Car lights outside, a horn.*)

ELLIE: What's that?

QUINCEY: (*At back door*) A car outside.

MARGO: A stranded motorist, probably. The roads must be slippery.

(*A voice calls,* "Ellie!")

ELLIE: (*At door*) Who is it?

VOICE: (*Offstage*) Ellie, I've been driving for hours. I thought I'd never find you. I know I should have called but I just couldn't. I hope you don't mind.

ELLIE: Peggy! (PEGGY's *at the door.*) Peggy!

(PEGGY *pours into* ELLIE's *arms.*)

PEGGY: I'm so glad to see you. I thought I was going to slide into a ditch, it's like driving on glass and my snow tires are old, they hardly have any tread. . . .

ELLIE: You look just the same.

PEGGY: You're lying. I look older.

ELLIE: A year or two.

PEGGY: (*Handing* ELLIE *her suitcase*) Here. Is it just terrible of me to come barging in?

ELLIE: No. Of course not.

PEGGY: I didn't have time to call. I walked out on Jim again. The second time this year. I just got in the car, I didn't know where I was going, then I remembered your letter was in my pocketbook, so I followed the directions and here I am. The directions were very good, I usually get lost a dozen times.

ELLIE: Come in.

PEGGY: Oh, you've got company. How stupid of me. I should have called, shouldn't I?

ELLIE: This is Pat, Quincey, Margo, Peggy.

PAT: Perfect Peggy. What do you know.

PEGGY: What?

PAT: Ellie used to talk about you—a lot. I called you Perfect Peggy. (*Pause.*) Forget it.

MARGO: Nice to meet you.

QUINCEY: Hi.

MARGO: Fortunately, we have plenty of food. Join us.

ELLIE: There's a guest bedroom, off to the right, upstairs. Can you manage that?

PEGGY: I managed to get it down the stairs, I guess I can get it up.

ELLIE: Make yourself comfortable, I'll be right up. (PEGGY *goes up the stairs. To* QUINCEY, PAT, MARGO) Can you handle everything down here?

PAT: I don't know. It's getting damned complicated.

MARGO: Go ahead. Five minutes till supper.

ELLIE: I'm sorry about all this, Margo.

MARGO: One has to learn to roll with the punches. I'm rather enjoying it; it's quite educational.

ELLIE: I'll figure something out.

MARGO: I'm sure you will.

    (MARGO *smiles as* ELLIE *mounts the stairs.*

    PAT *is at the window with* QUINCEY.)

PAT: The trouble with a late snow is—it's unexpected and messy as hell.

CURTAIN

ACT TWO

MARGO *is lying down in the living room, reading. Outside the noise of grinding gears and an occasional "Push!" "Rock it!" from* PAT *and* QUINCEY.

ELLIE *and* PEGGY *are in the kitchen, finishing dishes.*

It is dark outside.

PEGGY: . . . The first three or four years were good, Ellie. I had the kids, we bought the house, we had dreams. Jimmy was the bright young man in college, you remember.

ELLIE: I remember. "Most likely to succeed." Most popular girl weds boy "most likely."

PEGGY: Well, the world is full of colleges and every year thousands of young men, all of them "most likely," descend on the corporate world, swarming towards offices labeled "Executive Vice-President" like salmon dashing for the mating grounds. Head of Northeastern Sales is as far as Jimmy got.

ELLIE: That sounds impressive.

PEGGY: Not to Jimmy. It's a middle-management job. Nobody gets promoted from there. Jimmy says it's the slot reserved for failures. Eight years ago, he quit. He opened his own business. We borrowed from his folks and my folks and we took the kids' tuition money we'd saved—he opened a luxury hardware business.

ELLIE: Luxury hardware?

PEGGY: You know, fancy shelves, early American doorknobs, drawer pulls, drop latches, indirect lighting systems, self-stick bulletin boards, velvet contact paper.

ELLIE: Luxury hardware.

PEGGY: Jimmy has always been farsighted. The time was ripe. So many people living in apartments now, doing their own decorating.

ELLIE: Luxury hardware.

PEGGY: Listen, it was a good idea. Unfortunately, the manager of Woolworth's dime store across the street was also farsighted and sold the same merchandise for 8 percent less. Jimmy went back to Hamilton Die, Head of Northeastern Sales. He thinks of himself as a failure.

ELLIE: And you?

PEGGY: (*Not responding*) I've been working at a thrift shop downtown, four days a week. Lois is a senior this year. She wants to go to Bard but it's out of the question. They only give half scholarships. If she works this summer, between her salary and mine, we'll just be able to get her through a year at State.

ELLIE: You wanted a house on Mulhaven Drive with a maid and a garden out back. In the driveway . . .

PEGGY: (*Joining in the litany*) . . . the *circular* driveway . . .

ELLIE: . . . lined with towering elms . . .

PEGGY: . . . and paved with . . .

ELLIE: Gold.

PEGGY: No. Slate.

ELLIE: You'd sit in the late afternoon, your exquisite straw hat casting perfect shadows on your perfect features. . . .

PEGGY: . . . sipping tall, cool drinks . . .

ELLIE: . . . served on a silver tray, while planning that evening's formal dinner for the town dignitaries . . .

PEGGY: . . . and considering how someone in my position could help the less fortunate.

ELLIE: The fairy princess.

PEGGY: (*Laughing*) No. "Most popular girl weds boy most likely." I never got my circular drive: we have a carport—and a cleaning woman once a week.

ELLIE: Dreams rarely comes true.

PEGGY: Yours did. You wanted to teach in a university.

ELLIE: You thought it was a dull, old-maid thing to do.

PEGGY: And to live in a funky apartment with mobiles and wall hangings.

ELLIE: I do.

PEGGY: And to have a funny shack somewhere to get away from it all.

ELLIE: This is it.

PEGGY: Your dreams came true.

ELLIE: Not wholly. I wanted someone to share it with, someone to be a part of it, from the beginning to the end. I always wanted that.

PEGGY: Well, you can't have everything. You got the most important part.

ELLIE: Did I?

PEGGY: And you did it yourself. You didn't depend on someone else. I could never have done that.

ELLIE: Of course you could.

PEGGY: No. I could never have done that. (*She laughs.*) The curse of a fairy princess.

ELLIE: Remember how we used to go over the want ads on Sunday mornings. You were going to be a buyer for the fanciest store in town and I was going to teach. We'd live in a town house with high ceilings and hanging plants—

PEGGY: And mobiles and wall hangings? No, not me. That was you. I never wanted that.

ELLIE: Sometimes you did.

PEGGY: Never.

ELLIE: But the circular drive with the towering elms won out.

PEGGY: Actually, it's a development.

ELLIE: With a carport.

PEGGY: Yes. But it's my life. Mine and Jimmy's.

ELLIE: Why did you leave?

PEGGY: Eddie's at military school. Jim's father pays the tuition. "Make a man out of him." Frankly, I think it's making a jerk out of him. He's so damned disciplined, he doesn't know how to be a kid. Twelve years old and he gives orders like a five-star general. He won't stop at Head of Northeastern Sales.

ELLIE: Why did you leave, Peggy?

PEGGY: When a man thinks he's failed in business, he has to succeed somewhere. His job takes him on the road a lot so he has plenty of opportunity. I've never said a word about it, it's been going on for years. Oh, I haven't been lonely. I have a friend, Wanda. She works with me at the thrift shop. We go out to dinner and to the movies together. I've found letters from his girl friends and phone numbers in his wallet. He hasn't been home for a birthday or anniversary in years but I never accused him. I never accused him. How dare he accuse me!

ELLIE: Of having an affair?

PEGGY: How dare he?

ELLIE: Have you?

PEGGY: Why should he care if I did?

ELLIE: Did you?

PEGGY: He says, if you've thought about it, it's the same as doing it. I haven't done it!

ELLIE: You obviously want to.

PEGGY: Wanda thinks I should leave him.

ELLIE: What do you think?

PEGGY: I think he's a son of a bitch. I've put most of my life into this marriage. The kids will be out of school in a few years. I don't know. I don't know what I want. I guess that's why I came here. You're the only person I know who'll understand. You and Wanda.

ELLIE: (*Meaningfully*) Wanda?

PEGGY: You sound like Jim! Wanda is my friend, like you were my friend. I love her, like I loved you.

ELLIE: We loved each other—a step beyond friendship.

PEGGY: We were friends. Best friends. I never felt so close to anyone, until Wanda.

ELLIE: What you're feeling isn't friendship, Peggy. What we felt together wasn't friendship.

PEGGY: Of course it was! We loved each other.

ELLIE: We were in love with each other.

PEGGY: I'm not like that.

ELLIE: We made love.

PEGGY: That's not true!

ELLIE: Not often, we were both too scared. But we did make love. After the Saint Patrick's Party, New Year's Eve in New Hampshire, your birthday our senior year—I remember every time. I remember it because it was new and pure and perfect. It was always exciting, to the very end it was exciting. It was perfect.

PEGGY: You were going with Danny Rogers and I was going with Morton Tate—until the end of our senior year when I met Jim. We were good friends, Ellie. That's all. (*Pause.*)Danny Rogers is an assemblyman now. They say he's going to run for Congress. You missed a good bet. He married a mouse.

(*The door opens and* QUINCEY *and* PAT *enter, coats drenched from the snow.*)

QUINCEY: No luck.

PAT: We pushed and rocked and spun. It's already four inches and icing up. Nobody's going anywhere tonight.

PEGGY: Too bad Jim's not here. He could get it out.

ELLIE: You may not believe that this drunken women is an ace mechanic, but she is. If Pat can't move that car, nobody can.

PEGGY: I've always felt that men were just naturally better suited for some things.

QUINCEY: I don't believe I heard that.

PAT: (*Flirting with* PEGGY) She doesn't have a wart behind her ear. Has she been picking her nose?

PEGGY: What?

ELLIE: Never mind. Take off that wet coat, Quincey.

PAT: *(To* QUINCEY) Mind Mama. (*To* PEGGY) Want a drink?

PEGGY: Why not?

PAT: Follow me.

(*They go into living room.*)

MARGO: And?

PAT: Can't budge it. Want a drink?

MARGO: No, thanks. I've got coffee.

PAT: Party pooper. Now, what do you want, Perfect Peggy?

PEGGY: An after-dinner drink would be fine.

PAT: Ugh.

PEGGY: Creme de cocoa.

PAT: Really?

PEGGY: I like it.

PAT: I'll see if there's some in the kitchen. (*Goes to kitchen.*)

PEGGY: Excuse me. I hope you won't think I'm rude but . . . (MARGO *looks up.*) are you one of them?

MARGO: I beg your pardon?

PEGGY: You know. One of them.

MARGO: One of what?

PEGGY: Do you like men?

MARGO: Some men.

PEGGY: Do you sleep with them?

MARGO: Men?

PEGGY: Yes.

MARGO: I've probably slept with more men than you've ever met.

PEGGY: Oh, good. It looks like we're all going to have to stay over. You and I can share a room.

PAT: (*Entering with bottle*) That's the first proposition of the night.

PEGGY: (*About bottle, quickly*) That looks fine. That's a very good brand.

PAT: Nothing but the best, baby. Nothing but the best.

(*In the kitchen:*)

QUINCEY: Are you all right?

ELLIE: I'm worried.

QUINCEY: About Pat?

ELLIE: Who's going to be the victim. It's Pat's pattern. Step One: Seduce somebody. Step Two: Hurt somebody else by doing it. It's called "See how much everybody loves me? Anybody who loves me deserves to be punished."

QUINCEY: She wanted me to play a game with her.

ELLIE: A game?

QUINCEY: To pretend I was attracted to her, to Pat. It was supposed to make you pay attention to me.

ELLIE: (*Smiling*) I know that game. It's designed not to make me pay attention to you—but to her.

QUINCEY: I don't understand.

ELLIE: You're too honest. I hope you never understand.

QUINCEY: Something's happening and I'm frightened.

(*In the living room.*)

PEGGY: Are you really an auto mechanic?

PAT: Nope. I'm an antique dealer. A multifaceted human being.

PEGGY: I love antiques. Do you do appraisals?

PAT: Sure. Where do you live?

PEGGY: Oh, I'm too far. About seventy miles.

PAT: I travel.

PEGGY: Maybe you could recommend someone in my area.

PAT: You left your husband, huh?

PEGGY: I need some time to think things over.

PAT: You're bored.

PEGGY: I don't think so.

PAT: You're bored with him, with your marriage.

PEGGY: Maybe I am.

PAT: It happens to everybody. How long have you been bored?

PEGGY: (*Laughs.*) About ten years.

PAT: When the kids started school.

PEGGY: How do you know?

PAT: I've heard it before. I've known a few disgruntled wives.

PEGGY: I'm not just a disgruntled wife. There's a lot more to it.

PAT: There always is.

MARGO: (*Irritated, rises.*) Excuse me. (*She goes upstairs, into the bathroom.*)

PAT: Tell me about you and Ellie.

PEGGY: We were good friends.

PAT: She says you were the most beautiful girl in the school.

PEGGY: My daughter looks just like me. She's beautiful. (*Smiles.*) Things change.

PAT: You're probably more beautiful now.

PEGGY: You are drunk.

PAT: I think women get better with age. Like good wine . . .

PEGGY: Ellie got prettier. She was gawky in college. I never went through that gawky stage. I guess I'm going through it now.

PAT: She really loved you.

PEGGY: We were good friends.

PAT: Romeo and Juliet, Damon and Pythias, Jonathan and David, Gertrude and Alice . . .

PEGGY: We were good friends.

PAT: Nobody could ever live up to you.

PEGGY: No. We were friends. Not that I'm passing judgment on your lifestyle, but we were just friends.

PAT: That's all.

PEGGY: That's all.

PAT: Another creme de cocoa?

(*In the kitchen:*)

QUINCEY: Let's go to bed. Let's just go upstairs and go to bed and let them all do whatever it is that they're going to do.

ELLIE: I can't. When Pat is drunk, she not only plays her games — she's also likely to set the house on fire, turn on the gas without lighting it, leave the grate off the fireplace, fall through the storm door.

QUINCEY: I don't understand why you stayed with her for five years.

ELLIE: It wasn't always like this. Sometimes she'd go for months without drinking. When we were first together, she hardly drank at all. We were so happy and so much in love—and when the drinking started again, I knew what it could be like, what we could have together—and I kept hoping it would come back. I suppose I thought it was my fault.

QUINCEY: It wasn't.

ELLIE: No. It's just the way life is. The wind chimes stop.

QUINCEY: Wind chimes?

ELLIE: The excitement goes, the thrill, the lust, whatever you want to call it.

QUINCEY: But that's just the beginning. That's when a relationship starts: when you stop lusting and start loving.

ELLIE: Is it?

QUINCEY: You have to work at it.

ELLIE: How would you know? You've never had a relationship. You've gone from college affair to college affair.

QUINCEY: We're a relationship.

ELLIE: You've stopped lusting?

QUINCEY: (*Grins.*) Not entirely. When I first saw you at campus orientation, my knees shook. You were at a picnic table, hostessing. I sat down on the grass about twenty yards away and stared. I stared for two hours. For four years, I stared. You were my fantasy. When I finally got into a class of yours, my first grad year, your face was drawn and pained. Your hands shook. I wanted to run to the front of the room and hold you in my arms.

ELLIE: I remember that day. It was the day after the accident.

QUINCEY: I watched you fall apart that year, piece by piece—and piece by piece, put yourself back together: stronger. I loved you for five years before I made love to you. And even then, your thoughts were somewhere else. I know that. I don't care. You're mine now.

ELLIE: Quincey. Go on to bed, honey.

QUINCEY: Where?

ELLIE: In my room. I'll have to move Margo.

QUINCEY: You can't do that.

ELLIE: Would you rather sleep with Perfect Peggy?

QUINCEY: I'd rather sleep with you. In our room.

ELLIE: I'll be up as soon as I get Pat settled.

QUINCEY: Not too long.

ELLIE: At the rate she's drinking, she won't be able to stand up much longer.

   (QUINCEY *goes upstairs,* ELLIE *goes into living room.*)

PEGGY: Come on in, Ellie. Have a drink. Pat and I were discussing old times.

PAT: (*To* ELLIE) Your old times. (*To* PEGGY) Ellie doesn't drink.

PEGGY: I remember when she did. On the front porch of the frat house, you drank half a pint of Bourbon and did God-knows-what with Sammy Kincaid and while poor Danny was out beating the bushes for you.

ELLIE: That's why I don't drink.

PAT: Peggy says your college days together were right out of *A Date with Judy*—Jane Powell and Shirley Temple, giggling girl friends.

PEGGY: Well, Ellie did have a crush on me. I remember that. You were very jealous of Jim.

ELLIE: Of course I was!

PAT: And you used to give me the answers in Economics III. I only took that course because all the brightest boys did.

ELLIE: The most-likely-to-succeeds? (*Pause.*) Morty wanted to sleep with you and you told him you couldn't because you were in love with me.

PEGGY: He was a creep. I wanted to shock him.

ELLIE: He spread it all over the campus.

PEGGY: It was a kick. Well, it wasn't true. Anyone who knew me, knew that.

ELLIE: I didn't.

PEGGY: The jocks used to line up in the lounge to see me.

ELLIE: Yes. And Saint Patrick's night our sophomore year, you got into my bed.

PEGGY: I was drunk. I thought you were Jim.

ELLIE: You hadn't even met Jim then.

PEGGY: Well, I thought you were Morty.

PAT: Morty was a creep.

ELLIE: New Year's Eve. Remember New Year's Eve? You were engaged to Jim. At midnight, everybody kissed. You didn't kiss Jim. You kissed me. In front of the whole fucking fraternity house. Jim walked out. You didn't see him again until spring semester.

PEGGY: I didn't meet him until spring semester.

PAT: Will the real Perfect Peggy please stand up?

PEGGY: It didn't happen! Not like that.

ELLIE: It did. And it's happening again. With Wanda.

PEGGY: I'm not a lesbian! (*She runs upstairs to the guest bedroom, stage left.*)

PAT: It wasn't real.

ELLIE: It was!

PAT: Even if it happened, it wasn't real. Unadmitted, without commitment.

ELLIE: It was so perfect.

PAT: You never faced the bills together, you never faced joblessness together, you never built a house together, a life together. You never faced death together. It wasn't real. We were real.

ELLIE: We didn't work.

PAT: Why? I don't know why. I love you.

ELLIE: You don't love you.

PAT: All right. I never wanted to be a woman. It's a crappy thing to be. You can't do anything! I saw my father raking in the money, playing big business, flying to Europe, to the Caribbean, buying booze and women in every part of the globe while my mother ran the diaper brigade for eight kids. She never got farther than the corner A&P. Her conversation was limited to baby talk and what she heard on the radio. My father met Al Capone—met him! While my mother was scrubbing underwear on a washboard. Here's your choice, kiddies. Which one would you rather be?

ELLIE: Your father was a crook. What's good about that?

PAT: Is a crook. A successful one. The main man in Boston. My mother's dead of a heart attack.

ELLIE: I didn't know.

PAT: Last year.

ELLIE: I didn't know.

PAT: It doesn't matter. She's been dead for forty years. We finally buried her. But he goes on. And so do I. And I don't know why anymore. . . . Give us a chance, Ellie.

ELLIE: It's too late.

PAT: Can't you remember how it was? We built a home together: we made love on that beach at midnight and sailed that broken-down boat under the stars until dawn. We were safe from the world.

ELLIE: For a while.

PAT: Then you started teaching. You were gone so much, seeing new people. That's why I went out with other women, Ellie. To make you know how much you loved me.

ELLIE: The wind chimes stopped. And we didn't know how to make it work. Too much has happened. We can't go back.

PAT: Let me come home, Ellie.

ELLIE: I'm sorry. This isn't your home anymore.

(PAT *lunges for the front door and exits as* MARGO *comes down the stairs.*)

MARGO: (*To* PAT) Hey! It's cold out there. (*To* ELLIE) Shouldn't you go after her?

ELLIE: She's safer outside than in. She's very drunk, Margo. She'll wander around in the snow until she gets cold and wet enough to come in. As long as she can't move the car, she's safe.

MARGO: You know her very well.

ELLIE: I thought I did.

MARGO: Are you still in love with her? (ELLIE *turns, shocked.*) I'm not blind.

ELLIE: I'm sorry. I didn't intend to bring you into all of this.

MARGO: Are you?

ELLIE: I love her. I remember being in love with her. (*Pause.*) No.

MARGO: Quincey?

ELLIE: She loves me.

MARGO: That wasn't the question.

ELLIE: Quincey says that once the thrill goes, when the knees stop trembling and the wind chimes stop tinkling, it's a job. You've got to work at it.

MARGO: She's right.

ELLIE: Pat and I didn't know how to do that.

MARGO: But Quincey does.

ELLIE: Probably. But I think you have to hear chimes first.

MARGO: And you haven't?

ELLIE: Not with Quincey. I love her. I appreciate her, I'm thankful for her. But no chimes. Ever.

MARGO: I was married to a man once, much like Pat. Worse, I guess. He was not only a drunk but a violent drunk. And I loved him. I loved him long after I left him. And I loved again. A woman. She died ten years ago.

ELLIE: (*Surprised*) I'm sorry.

MARGO: I haven't written a publishable book since that time. I haven't let another human being touch me since that time. Oh, I've slept with a few. I picked up a salesman in the bar downstairs from my hotel room. He was from Detroit. I never saw him again. Another time, a bellhop. And a woman reporter from a newspaper upstate. She was in town for the afternoon to interview me. But they didn't touch me: not emotionally, not really physically. I made love to them. . . . It's hard to make anything last, Ellie. A job, a talent, a marriage.

ELLIE: A lot of people do it.

MARGO: A lot of people hold on to dead things. But to make something last—and live . . . It's harder with a woman. There are no rules. And the stakes are so very high. (*They look at each other for a moment.*) We worked at it. We worked very hard at it. We brought new things into our relationship, we challenged one another with ideas, with goals. We weren't always successful. We had bad years, years when I was sure it was over, when I thought it should be over. But we survived them, somehow. It was good again, it was working. (*Pause.*) I think I hated her for dying, for leaving me. And I was very frightened. I still am.

ELLIE: But you've learned to be alone.

MARGO: I don't do it very well. I need to share, to be a part of something.

ELLIE: But they don't last. It doesn't last. You start to build—and it's over. You start again—and it's over. Why bother?

MARGO: Because you need it. I need it. And we keep hoping, all of us: men and women, women and women, men and men, that we can make it work. What do you want, Ellie?

ELLIE: Someone to grow with. Someone to build with.

MARGO: You can do that with Quincey. What do you want, Ellie?

ELLIE: I want it all. I want to tremble. I want that kind of crazy desire that surmounts reason. I want someone to live for, to die with. Someone to climb mountains for, slay dragons for, someone to snuggle with by a fire when the world is cold. I want a lover consumed by the greatest passion, a partner possessed of the greatest loyalty, a friend committed to the greatest love.

With Pat, there was passion. With Quincey, there is loyalty. I don't want to settle. I want it all.

I thought I'd had it all with Peggy. Passion, loyalty, friendship. I thought it had been perfect. But it was so long ago and I was so young. I knew less than. Maybe I needed less, too.

MARGO: Does she remember it as perfect?

ELLIE: She doesn't remember it at all.

(QUINCEY *appears at the head of the stairs.*)

QUINCEY: Are you coming up?

ELLIE: In a minute.

(QUINCEY *comes down the stairs.*)

QUINCEY: Where's Pat?

MARGO: She's outside. Waiting for spring.

QUINCEY: Is she all right?

ELLIE: I want to wait and see. Go back to bed, honey. I'll be up in a minute.

QUINCEY: Okay. Hurry. (*She goes back up the stairs.*)

MARGO: What are you going to do, Ellie?

ELLIE: I don't want to hurt anybody.

MARGO: Why did you ask me here?

ELLIE: (*Pause.*) Because I liked you.

MARGO: Liked me?

ELLIE: Because I felt something. The night we talked in my hotel room, I felt something.

MARGO: What?

ELLIE: I don't know. Something. A beginning.

MARGO: And what are you going to do about it?

ELLIE: (*Pause.*) Wait.

MARGO: Why?

ELLIE: Because I'm scared. Because I'm tonguetied when I talk to you, and my knees feel weak. When I stand near you there's electricity between us like a living thing. Because something great is growing here and I'm afraid for it to start. I don't want it to end. And I don't know what you want.

MARGO: (*After a long moment*) I want you. (*Holds out her arms.*) Don't settle, Ellie.

(ELLIE *goes into* MARGO's *arms as* PAT *comes quietly in the back door, wet and drunken. She see what is happening and sneaks quietly up the stairs to* PEGGY's *room.* PEGGY *is staring out the window at the lake.*)

PAT: Hi, there.

PEGGY: It's the abominable snowman.

PAT: The boat has a hole in it.

(*From the bedroom:*)

QUINCEY: Ellie?

(*In the living room:*)

ELLIE: (*To* MARGO) I've got to go.

MARGO: Not yet.

(*Upstairs:*)

PAT: (*Crossing the hallway to* QUINCEY's *room*) Hi.

QUINCEY: Hi.

PAT: (*Explaining*) The boat has a hole in it.

QUINCEY: What?

PAT: Ellie wants you downstairs.

(QUINCEY *gets up as* PAT *goes back to* PEGGY's *room.*)

PEGGY: Don't sit on the bed. You're all wet.

PAT: You want me to take them off?

PEGGY: No!

(*Downstairs:*)

MARGO: You've got to make a decision, Ellie.

(*Upstairs:*)

PAT: I will if you will.

PEGGY: Stop it! (*She starts to cry.*)

PAT: Hey, I'm sorry.

(*Downstairs:*)

MARGO: I have something at stake here, too, you know. I have everything at stake.

(*Upstairs:*)

PAT: Come on, cut the waterworks.

PEGGY: Hold me. Please hold me. I'm so afraid.

PAT: (*Doing it*) Perfect Peggy.

(QUINCEY *comes down the stairs, unsuspectingly turns the corner.*)

QUINCEY: Ellie? (*She sees* ELLIE *and* MARGO. *Turns, runs up the stairs.*)

ELLIE: Quincey!

QUINCEY: No! (*She runs into the room, slams and locks the door.* ELLIE *follows.*)

ELLIE: Quincey! Quincey?

QUINCEY: No!

MARGO: (*At the foot of the stairs*) Leave her alone, Ellie.

(ELLIE *slowly comes down the steps. As the lights in the upstairs room dim to black. ELLIE and MARGO move to the sofa in the firelight. They lie down together and the firelight slowly dims then cross fades to dawn.*)

PAT: Rise and shine! (QUINCEY *in her room and* PEGGY *in hers hear and rise and hurriedly begin to dress.*) The birds are chirping, the sun is shining and the late snow is melting into spring.

MARGO: (*Sitting up*) Why aren't you hung over?

ELLIE: (*Sleepily*) She never is.

MARGO: It's criminal.

PAT: Rise and shine, Ellie, put on the coffee! We itinerants have to get packing.

MARGO: Make it yourself, you chauvinist pig.

ELLIE: Believe me, you wouldn't want to drink it.

(PAT*'s in the kitchen, getting the pot out.*)

PAT: The pot, coffee, measuring cup: all ready! (ELLIE *rises, goes to the kitchen.* PAT *countercrosses to the living room. To* MARGO) Sleep well?

MARGO: Fine, thank you. What about you? Did you sleep in the snow?

PAT: I came in. (*Pause.*) Upstairs with Perfect Peggy.

MARGO: You're very sure of yourself, aren't you?

PAT: Not at all. I know what I want.

MARGO: Not Peggy.

PAT: Not Peggy. . . . I'm a gambler. Are you?

MARGO: No.

PAT: I can tell. Your odds are bad. She's a three-time loser. And I know the track. Are you betting win, place, or show?

MARGO: Across the board.

PAT: Want some advice?

MARGO: No.

PAT: Come back to town with me. I'll take you to dinner, we'll get to know each other. I'm a very interesting person.

MARGO: (*Smiles.*) No.

PAT: I'd make a great character for a book. You can study me.

MARGO: (*Smiles.*) No.

PAT: I can't take you out of the running, huh?

MARGO: (*Smiles.*) No.

(ELLIE *has put on the coffee and goes upstairs. She knocks on* QUINCEY*'s door.*)

ELLIE: Quincey?

PAT: I'm going out to start the car. But I'm not going far. Ever.

(*Upstairs:*)

ELLIE: Quincey.

(QUINCEY *unlocks the door, admits* ELLIE.

Downstairs:)

PAT: Consider yourself warned.

(*Upstairs:*)

ELLIE: Quincey.

QUINCEY: That's why you brought her here.

ELLIE: No.

QUINCEY: It wasn't enough in Philadelphia.

ELLIE: That's not how it happened.

QUINCEY: And Chicago and Des Moines and how many other cities, how many other conferences, how many other business trips? I've been sitting home like an idiot, believing you.

ELLIE: It never happened before.

QUINCEY: What was I? A convenient place to rest?

ELLIE: I wanted it to work with us, Quincey.

QUINCEY: You never worked at it. My whole life is constructed around you. I can't write what I want to, it reflects on you. I can't be who I am, you'll lose your job. "May I ask someone home for supper?

May I have the key to the cabin? May I use the car? May I, may I, may I?" Ellie decides everything. What Ellie wants, what Ellie needs, how Ellie wants to live. I don't even exist!

ELLIE: I'm sorry.

QUINCEY: Sorry isn't good enough! You made a commitment to me!

ELLIE: I didn't want to. Do you remember that? I didn't want to.

QUINCEY: I thought you'd learn to love me.

ELLIE: I wanted to. I really wanted to.

QUINCEY: We're good together!

ELLIE: No. It isn't enough, Quincey. It's bad for me—it's bad for you. You have so much love to give.

QUINCEY: I love you.

ELLIE: I love you. But not the right way.

QUINCEY: Is this just an affair? A week? A month? I'll wait.

ELLIE: No.

QUINCEY: I'm good for you.

ELLIE: But I'm not good for you. You're young, you can be free, you can be open, you can build the kind of life you want. You can fight for what you believe in. You can make a difference, Quincey. There's a world of women out there, young women, who'll stand with you.

QUINCEY: I want you.

ELLIE: I can't.

QUINCEY: Are you in love with her?

ELLIE: I don't know yet. I think so.

QUINCEY: Then you're not in love with me. You've never been in love with me. (*Pause.*) I guess I've always known that. I thought I could make it happen.

ELLIE: I never lied to you.

QUINCEY: Not in words. By holding me, living with me, making love to me. You lied to me. (*She hits the wind chimes at the window.*) I heard them. You didn't. You used me. That's the most degrading part of all.

ELLIE: I'm sorry.

QUINCEY: I have some sweaters and things in the drawers. I'd like to pack them. (*Pause.*) Can I use that duffel bag?

ELLIE: (*Nods. Going to her.*) Quincey . . .

QUINCEY: (*Pulling away*) For God's sake, leave me with some dignity.

(ELLIE *backs from the room, watching* QUINCEY *for a moment, then closes the door.*

PEGGY *comes out of the bathroom, dressed.*)

PEGGY: Good morning. (*She goes into her bedroom, gets her suitcase.*) Ready to go. Hope I can get my car out.

ELLIE: You're leaving?

PEGGY: I'm going home.

ELLIE: Oh.

PEGGY: I have a life there. It's not what I had in mind, but it's mine.

ELLIE: With Jim?

PEGGY: He won't change. Neither can I.

ELLIE: And Wanda?

PEGGY: Wanda is my friend. That's all. That's the way it's going to stay. I can't deal with it, Ellie. It takes courage: a kind I haven't got.

ELLIE: You came here for help. I'm afraid I didn't offer much.

PEGGY: I came looking for an answer. An answer that worked for me. I found it. I have a nice house, two lovely children, a good job. I'll settle for that. (*She proceeds down the stairs with her suitcase.*)

(PAT *enters from the yard.*)

PAT: Car's started. We'll have no problem getting out.

PEGGY: What about mine?

PAT: It's only a couple of feet from the road.

PEGGY: Would you do it for me?

PAT: My pleasure.

PEGGY: Now.

PAT: Don't you want a cup of coffee first?

PEGGY: I'll stop on the road. I want to go home. Before I change my mind. (*She extends her hand.*) Ellie, thanks. Don't go to any more New Year's Eve parties. It gets everybody in a lot of trouble.

(PEGGY *and* PAT *exit.*

QUINCEY *comes down the stairs, carrying the duffel bag. She and* ELLIE *look at one another for a minute.*)

QUINCEY: I want the apartment. I decorated it and I want it.

ELLIE: (*Meekly*) All right.

QUINCEY: Call me when you want to pick up your things. I won't be there. (*She pauses, looks at the Dutch cupboard, touches it.*) To remember me by. (*She looks at* MARGO.) I suppose I'll see you around campus. (*She crosses to the door.*) Work at it. (*She exits.*)

ELLIE: Will we have this moment?

MARGO: There are no guarantees.

ELLIE: Perfect Peggy settled.

MARGO: Some people have to. (*Pause.*) And some people can't.

(ELLIE *pours a cup of coffee and hands it to* MARGO.)

ELLIE: The snow's almost gone.

(PAT *enters brightly, takes the coffee out of* MARGO's *hand, sips it.*)

PAT: Thanks. Well, Peggy's on her way. You always had good taste, Ellie. (*She pockets a piece of paper.*) Her phone number. She needs an occasional appraisal. (*She gulps the rest of* MARGO's *coffee, hands her the empty cup.*) Quincey's waiting in the car.

ELLIE: Thanks for delivering the hutch.

PAT: It's okay. I overcharged her. (*To* MARGO) Across the board?

MARGO: Across the board.

PAT: I'll be waiting at the finish line. (*She kisses* ELLIE *on the cheek.*) See you soon, Ellie.

ELLIE: No.

PAT: (*Shaking* MARGO's *hand*) Good luck.

MARGO: We're running on a long track, Pat.

PAT: I've got a lot of patience.

    (PAT *exits.*

    ELLIE *watches them go.*

    MARGO *pours two cups of coffee.*)

MARGO: Black?

ELLIE: Fine.

MARGO: (*Gives the coffee to* ELLIE.) Where will you live?

ELLIE: I'll find an apartment.

MARGO: I'll need to live near campus. How would that look, our living together?

ELLIE: Do you care?

MARGO: No.

ELLIE: Neither do I. I'm tired of living a half-life.

MARGO: So am I.

ELLIE: I can't march. But I won't hide. (*She moves to window.*) What's your favorite color?

MARGO: Blue.

ELLIE: Favorite flower?

MARGO: Marigold.

ELLIE: Favorite season?

MARGO: Summer.

ELLIE: Favorite food?

MARGO: Pineapple.

ELLIE: Pineapple?

MARGO: (*Smiling*) Pomegranate?

(*Both are at the window.*)

ELLIE: The snow is gone. The sun is out. (*She opens the window.*) Favorite person? (*The wind chimes tinkle in the breeze. They both laugh.* MARGO *holds out her arms.*) Let's try to keep it that way. (*The lights fade in the foreground until the two women are silhouetted in the morning sun.*)

CURTAIN

JANE CHAMBERS (1937-1983) began her career in the late 1950s as an actress and playwright, working Off-Broadway and in coffeehouse theatre. Her plays have been produced Off-Broadway, in regional theatres, community theatres and on television. She has been the recipient of the Connecticut Educational Television Award (1971/*Christ in a Treehouse*), a Eugene O'Neill fellowship (1972/*Tales of the Revolution and Other American Fables*), a National Writer's Guild Award (1973/*Search for Tomorrow,* CBS), the Dramalogue Critics Circle Award, the Villager Theatre Award, the Alliance for Gay Artists Award and the Robby Award (1981, 1983-4/*Last Summer at Bluefish Cove*, N.Y. and L.A. productions) and the Fund for Human Dignity Award (1982), among others. She was a founding member of the New Jersey Women's Political Caucus and of the Interart Theatre in Manhattan, and a member of the Planning Committee of the Women's Program of the American Theatre Association. She was also a member of the Writer's Guild East, the Dramatists Guild, the Author's League, Actors Equity and the East End Gay Organization for Human Rights. On February 15, 1983, she died of a brain tumor at her Greenport, Long Island home; she is survived by her mother, Clarice, her two step-brothers, Henry and Ben, and her life's companion, Beth Allen. The Women In Theatre Program (formerly the American Theatre Association, Women's Division) has created the Jane Chambers Playwriting Award to encourage the writing of new plays which address women's experience and have a majority of principal roles for women.

ALSO AVAILABLE FROM JH PRESS

Jane Chambers' **BURNING**   (ISBN 0-935672-10-9) $6.95

A lesbian gothic suspense novel! Jane Chambers has written a tale of love that transcends time: Cynthia desperately needed a break from the city and took the offer of a vacation home, sight unseen. Hiring Angela, a young woman who lived in the same apartment building, to help with the children, Cynthia took possession of the New England farmhouse. And then, from an earlier century, Abigail and Martha reached out to possess the living.

> "Burning *brings the past persecution of lesbians into the present in an illuminating tale that is both an affirmation of a way of life and a good suspense story. I loved reading it."*
> — SANDRA SCOPPETTONE

Jane Chambers' **WARRIOR AT REST**   (ISBN 0-935672-12-5) $5.95

Jane Chambers was widely known as a playwright and novelist, but she was also an accomplished poet. The poems in this collection were written from 1958 to 1983, and cover experiences from her life at Goddard College and working in the Job Corps in Maine and New Jersey to the impact of terminal illness in the last months of her life. These poems are personal responses to specific events and feelings, expressed in imagery often too enigmatic to be incorporated into a novel or play.

> "Whimsical, sad, often funny, always affecting ... treasured glimpses into the heart and humanity of this gifted woman."
> —THE ADVOCATE

ALSO AVAILABLE FROM JH PRESS

Jane Chambers' CHASIN JASON   ISBN 0-935672-13-3
$9.95

With this work, Chambers has created a startling book that defies genre classification. A science fiction novel about the second coming of Christ, but told in a wry first-person narrative by his foster mother, the book is as futuristic as it is folksy, as high-tech as it is humorous.

> "A very funny and totally unique book."
> —BAY WINDOWS

> "A fascinating book to read—both entertaining and thought-provoking."
> —THE WEEKLY NEWS

C. D. Arnold's THE DINOSAUR PLAYS
(ISBN 0-935672-09-5) $5.95

Three one-act plays by the popular West Coast playwright: "A Night in the Blue Moon," concerns the futility of re-creating adolescent romance; "The Blonde in Twenty-B," a lesbian love triangle; and "Dinosaurs," about a proud street queen and his ex-hustler dolt of a boyfriend.

> "A talented playwright. . . . Arnold's voice is not unlike Tennessee Williams, though in no imitative sense: he shares with Williams strong passion, an ability to write very sensuously and a sense of identification with the victims of our society."
> —SAN FRANCISCO BAY GUARDIAN

Doric Wilson's **STREET THEATER** (ISBN 0-935672-07-9) $6.95

Written especially for San Francisco's Theatre Rhinoceros, *Street Theater* concerns Christopher Street in the hours leading up to the Stonewall Riots. It focuses on a panorama of lesbians, drag queens, leathermen, flower children, vice cops and cruisers— the innocent and not-so-innocent bystanders who would turn the 27th of June, 1969 into D-Day in gay history.

> *"A milestone . . . the audience stood applauding long and hard."*
>
> —THE ADVOCATE

> *"One of the best gay plays around."*
> —BAY AREA REPORTER

Terry Miller's **PINES '79**   (ISBN 0-935672-06-0) $5.95

Terry Miller compacts all the "frantic relaxation" of a Fire Island summer into two hilarious hours. The *New York Native* reports: "They're all here: the lovers who never stop fighting, the dealer who runs out of the drug he himself craves, the businessman who swears every summer is his last on Fire Island, and the kid from the sticks who actually has intentions of spending a summer in the Pines and not getting corrupted."

> *"An engaging, often very funny play that provokes ample laughter."*
>
> —BACKSTAGE

> *"Viewed as good fun, liberal straights would enjoy its easy laughs."*
> —OTHER STAGES

ALSO AVAILABLE FROM JH PRESS

Jane Chambers' **MY BLUE HEAVEN** (ISBN 0-935672-6) $5.95

The parson comes a-calling on the "Farm Couple of the Year," Molly and Josie, two lovers who leave sophisticated Manhattan to rough it in upstate New York, but he finds that everything's gay in *My Blue Heaven*, Jane Chambers' latest comedy, written especially for the Second Gay American Arts Festival, presented by The Glines in June 1981. In two of the "Adventures of Molly and Jo," a Christian book publisher wants to publish Molly's fictionalized version of her and Josie's life together in book form, and later, Molly and Josie are visited by a childhood sweetheart of Molly's who is now a minister and wants them to marry to prove how "progressive" he is.

> *"One of the funniest, most life-affirming comedies to hit New York in the past decade."*
> —N.Y. DAILY NEWS

> *"Josie and Molly['s] . . . relationship is as individual, as rich and as difficult as most intense and sexual relationships."*
> —NEWSDAY

Doric Wilson's **FOREVER AFTER** (ISBN 0-935672-01-X) $5.95

Doric Wilson's latest hit comedy was written especially for the First Gay American Arts Festival presented in June 1980 by The Glines. The author describes it as "a crazy, free-form, free-wheeling, irreverent, even libelous, vivisection of gay male love, lovers, life and theatre."

> *"Hilarious . . . sheer fun . . . it may well live in the theatre forever after."*
> —SOHO NEWS

> *"Brimming with acid wisecracks and neat farcical business."*
> —VILLAGE VOICE

ALSO AVAILABLE FROM JH PRESS

Arch Brown's **NEWS BOY**   (ISBN 0-935672-02-8) $3.95

News Boy was first presented in 1979 by The Glines, moved Off-Broadway in 1980 and has subsequently been performed by the Gay Theatre of New York (GAYTONY) in a national tour. It is a love story, "honest, direct, caring," set against the current political climate. Tim is coming out only to be confronted by his mother running for senator on an anti-gay platform. What was private and personal is suddenly on the six o'clock news.

> *"Slick, fast-paced and funny, getting to the heart of important gay issues."*
> —MANDATE

GAY THEATRE ALLIANCE DIRECTORY OF GAY PLAYS
compiled and edited and with an introduction by Terry Helbing
(ISBN 0-935672-00-1) $5.95

The first reference book on gay theatre presents comprehensive information on 400 plays relevant to lesbians and gay men. Listings for each play include complete production, publication and script information and the book is designed to be a practical, useful guide for theatre practitioners, gay people and anyone interested in gay theatre, past and present.

> *"A large first step toward recording the history of homosexuality in dramatic literature."*
> —GOTHAM

> *"Nicely organized . . . a well-done work, recommended for most theatre collections."*
> —LIBRARY JOURNAL

ALSO AVAILABLE FROM JH PRESS

Jane Chambers' **LAST SUMMER AT BLUEFISH COVE**
Paperback: (ISBN 0-935672-05-2) $6.95
Special hardcover limited edition; numbered, signed and with an introduction by the author relating her own experience with cancer: (ISBN 0-935672-04-4) $25.00

Heralded by audiences and critics alike as the "breakthrough lesbian play," Jane Chambers' *Last Summer at Bluefish Cove* is a tender and moving but still hilariously funny portrait of a tightly knit summer community of long-time lesbian friends. For one of the women, it is her last summer there, because of her struggle with terminal cancer. She meets and falls in love with a woman to whom she can bequeath her special gifts of warmth, spirit and independence.

> *"A funny, touching, surprisingly upbeat and enlightened portrait of female homosexuality . . . a landmark event."*
>
> —OTHER STAGES

> *"A tight, truthful script by turns wonderfully funny and painfully sad, that holds its own with the best writing around town today."*
>
> —N.Y. DAILY NEWS